Everything You Need to Know About …

Writing Songs - Simplified

Helen Iles

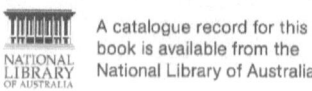

A catalogue record for this book is available from the National Library of Australia

Copyright © 2025 Helen Iles
All Song Lyrics © 2025 Helen Iles
All rights reserved.
ISBN-13: 978-1-923174-62-7

Linellen Press
265 Boomerang Road
Oldbury, Western Australia
www.linellenpress.com.au

Dedication

To all my friends for your encouragement
as I shuffled from the role of a Poet
into the land of the Lyricist.

Contents

Dedication iii
Contents v
Introduction 1
So, What is a Song? 5
The Songwriting Process: 6
Lyric Writing Techniques 11
Melody Creation: 21
Finding Inspiration for Songwriting 27
Collaboration in Songwriting 31
The Importance of Structure 36
in Songwriting 36
Defining Your Style 47
Using Technology in Songwriting 51
Overcoming Writer's Block 55
Analysing Successful Tunes 58
The Role of Emotion in Songs 61
Performing Your Songs 68
Self-Publishing and Promotion 73
for Songwriters 73
Songwriting Challenges 77
Building a Songwriting Community 84
Examples of Lyrical Inspiration 89
Finale 103
About the Author 104

Introduction

Music gives a soul to the universe, wings to the mind, flight to the imagination and life to everything.

Plato

Musical training is a more potent instrument than any other, because rhythm and harmony find their way into the inward places of the soul.

Plato

Music produces a kind of pleasure which human nature cannot do without.

Confucius

What better way to start a book than with pertinent quotes from the world's most prominent philosophers about music, statements I wholeheartedly agree with. But when it comes to my relationship to music, I come closest to the quote by world-renowned physicist Albert Einstein, who said:

If I were not a physicist, I would probably be a musician. I often think in music. I live my daydreams in music. I see my life in terms of music.

In my case, if I were not a poet, I would probably be a musician. I often think in music. I live my daydreams in music. I see my life in terms of music. Yet I am not a musician. I am a writer and a poet, yet I hear music in the words I write, and I see stories in the music I hear. Often, my novels have a music score running behind the scenes I create that only I can hear. Oh, if only I could play an instrument to bring that music to life.

Many years ago, when a good friend mentioned I should put one of my award-winning poems to music, the thought bubbled away for a few years before I started wondering how that could happen. My fear was that, if I offered my poem to a musician to turn it into a song, the end result might not be even close to the music I could hear within the words I wrote. So I sat on it, protectively, possessively, until …

Wait for it! …

I am a firm believer that things always happen for a reason – my friend's suggestion was one of those things – the planting of the seed that music might blossom from a poem. I am also a firm believer that good things will happen when the time is right – you just have to be patient. I am also a person who hates waste, and when going through a wad of rhyming poetry, clearing space for other things, I was loath to destroy something I had enjoyed producing simply because rhyming poetry had lost its popularity over the years when free verse and experimental writing was deemed more emotive and complex in its composition, and therefore, more valued. I then shrivelled under the embarrassment of being a 'rhyming poet' and joined the ranks of being a non-rhyming poet. Yet I could no longer hear the music in my words.

While listening to music as I decluttered my house, my treasured book of bush ballads in my hand heading for the disposal chute, my friend's words came back to me – it seems I was in the right place at the right time! The songs! The songs that were playing … the songs I was enjoying and singing along with were … rhyming. Epiphany! Light bulb moment! Turn my poems into songs! Decluttering had happened at the right time, and had happened for a reason! I was in tune with the tune. There would be no wastage of rhyme, time or reason!

And so, my sojourn into writing song lyrics began. As a creative writing coach for many years, it didn't take long to learn the requirements of a good song, to replicate the style of song I loved to sing along with, and start converting my poems to song lyrics, and then developing song lyrics anew. These processes have been included in the book as I take several songs from scratch and show how the lyrics developed, were inspired, or were derived from poems, and the process of taking them through to the final product, ready for release to the world.

Come and join me on my lyrical journey. And start yours.

So, What is a Song?

As a storyteller/novelist, I know a good story is one that resonates with readers by evoking their emotions through events and effective development of the characters involved in the story, with a depth of writing that allows the reader/listener to escape from reality into the story.

A good song is no different. The lyrics should evoke emotions and connect with listeners through their conversational style and create further emotive responses through the effective use of the musical elements of melody, harmony and rhythm, which should match the mood of the story and the impact of the action on the character the song is about. Each element needs to be well-crafted to ensure a memorable and relatable experience for the listener, ultimately leaving them with a lasting impression that makes them want to hear the song again and again.

The Songwriting Process:

The Very Quick Basics

Songwriting is a creative discipline that involves a skillful blend of inspiration, imagination, and technique. While every songwriter/lyricist has their own distinct method of creating songs, here is a comprehensive overview of the typical steps involved in writing a song, from brainstorming ideas to crafting melodies and refining lyrics. These steps will be covered in more depth in later chapters.

1. Brainstorming Ideas

- **Inspiration:** Begin by collecting inspiration from a variety of sources. This may include personal experiences, emotions, social themes, or even tales from others. Keep a journal or a notes application handy to capture spontaneous ideas, or jot down your thoughts in a spreadsheet.

- **Theme Selection:** Pick a theme or emotion that resonates with you. This could be, for instance, love, heartbreak, empowerment, or nostalgia. A strong theme often acts as the backbone for your song.

2. Creating a Concept

- **Song Structure**: Decide on the structure of your song. Common structures include:
- Verse-Chorus-Verse,
- Verse-Verse-Bridge-Verse
- Verse, Chorus, Verse, Chorus, Bridge, Verse, Chorus
- or even more experimental formats.

This will help establish the flow of your song.

- **Title Development**: Consider a title that captures the essence of your song. A catchy title can also guide the direction of your lyrics.

3. Draft the Lyrics

- **Verse Writing**: Begin writing your verses, laying out the narrative or message you want to convey. Focus on creating vivid imagery and relatable messages to engage your audience.

- **Chorus Creation**: Write the chorus, which is often the emotional centrepiece of the song. It should be catchy and memorable, capturing the essence of your theme.

- **Bridge/Hook**: If your song incorporates a bridge, this is an opportunity to present a contrasting idea or shift in the story perspective. It can add depth and interest to your song.

If I have an idea for a song, I might even write the whole story in full, developing characters and events and the twist in the tale, if it has one. Then I identify what parts of the story are the verses, the chorus and bridge, the twist in the tale usually becoming the Outro.

4. Composing Melodies

- **Melody Creation**: Hum or play around on an instrument to find a melody that fits with your lyrics. Experiment with different notes and rhythms until you find a tune that resonates with the mood of your song.

(If you do not play an instrument, this is an opportune time to collaborate with a musician to help create the music and/or vocals.

- **Chords and Harmonies**: Once you have a melody, start adding chords to complement it. This will enhance the emotional impact of the song. Don't hesitate to experiment with different chord progressions.

5. Refinement and Revision

- **Edit Lyrics**: Go back through your lyrics and refine them to match the melody. Look for any phrases that feel awkward or forced. Aim for clarity and emotional authenticity.

- **Feedback**: Share your song with trusted friends or fellow musicians. Listen to their feedback, as it may provide valuable insights or inspire further changes

6. Arrangement

- **Instrumentation**: Consider the arrangement of your song. What instruments will enhance the overall sound? Think about where to place each element to create dynamics and build tension.

- **Structure Finessing**: Revisit your song structure and make adjustments if needed. Ensure that the flow feels natural and engaging from start to finish.

7. Finalising the Song

- **Practice**: Perform your song multiple times, (or listen to it being played) paying attention to delivery and emotional impact. Make small adjustments to strengthen words, phrasing and dynamics as needed.

- **Recording**: If you're ready, consider recording a demo. This doesn't have to be a professional-quality recording; a simple setup can capture the essence of your song.

For lyricists, this is definitely a time to consider hiring musicians to perform your song, or songs, or approach a Songwriting Service that can assist with this. These services can be found on the internet, but check out their reviews, charges, number of amendments allowed, and percentage of royalties they require for their service and compare them to others in the industry. Working with local artists may be of greater benefit for working collaboratively face-to-face.

Conclusion

The songwriting process can be a deeply personal and rewarding experience. While following these steps can provide a solid framework, remember that creativity knows no strict rules. Don't be afraid to embrace spontaneity, experiment and allow your unique voice to shine through.

Lyric Writing Techniques

Let's dive a little deeper into the process of writing lyrics.

Writing lyrics is an art form that combines creativity with emotional depth, allowing songwriters to convey messages, tell stories, and evoke feelings. Here, we explore various approaches to lyric writing, including storytelling, imagery, and emotional expression.

1. Storytelling

One of the most powerful techniques in lyric writing is storytelling. Every compelling song often has a narrative that draws listeners in and keeps them engaged. And it is only a brief episode, not a full-blown novel.

Here are some elements to consider when crafting a story through your lyrics:

- **Character Development**: Introduce characters or personas your listeners can relate to, that is, strike a chord (excuse the pun) with their own life experiences. Describe the character's journeys, conflicts, and transformations. This helps listeners connect on a personal level, and more so if they have had a similar experience.

Just like writing a novel, you need to craft your song's characters so listeners can feel for them; feel their pain. They have a life before the song, and they will have a life after it, yet most of this is implied. You, however, will need to know what that 'before' and 'after' is to be able to input the right amount of emotion into your story. You need to feel what your character feels for this emotion to come through in your words. Hence, writing about your own life experiences will let the emotions come through most clearly.

- **Plot Structure**: Like any good story, your lyrics should have a clear beginning, middle, and end. Establish the setting, build tension, and lead to a resolution or climax. In the Introductory verse (often called Intro), I like to reveal the scene, showing time and place and the main character and issue of the story.

For example: in *Nomadic Dream*, the opening lines are:

> *Red dust on my boots, a wide map in my mind*
> *Chasing glorious sunsets, leaving troubles behind*

From this, the implied story reveals the singer is walking on red dusty trails, the wide map in their mind showing they have no limits to where they might be going; they are prepared to keep moving towards each new sunset, and the further they go, the more distant they will be from whatever conflict set them drifting from home in the first place. While you don't explain all that, the story is implied and let's the listener use their own imagination to fill in the detail.

- **Conflict and Resolution**: Incorporating a central conflict adds depth to the story. It can be an internal struggle, a relationship challenge, or a broader social issue. The resolution can offer closure or action-oriented messages.

The repeated Chorus throughout the 'story'

> *Now I'm a drifter, my heart wide open,*
> *Rolling like the wind, resolve never broken,*
> *Stars are my compass, freedom my home,*
> *On the stretch of this road, I'll never be alone.*

indicates the singer is moving forward with their life with a positive outlook with no intention of returning, stated in 'resolve never broken' to have an open heart and keep rolling like the wind.

The conflict in the story is an implied relationship breakdown that has created a 'new beginning' story as the second verse shows:

Cities glimmer by in a brightly blurred hue,

While campfire embers scatter my thoughts of you,

In strangers' smiles, there's a warmth I can find,

In those fleeting moments, I leave the past behind.

And in the final verse (the Outro), the resolution occurs:

A new life begins as all thoughts of you die,

Drifting down this long highway, a new love I'll find

For the road is heart's healer and I leave the past behind.

My freedom's heart's healer and I leave all memories of you behind.

Released in May 2025 on the Album 'These Country Boots'

- **Dialogue**: Integrating conversation between characters can provide authenticity and immediacy. It also breaks up the lyrical flow and can add dynamic energy to the song.

There is no dialogue exchange in *Nomadic Dream* as the singer is telling the listener their thoughts directly. Though there is a twist to the song that will leave the listener contemplating, which is also a good technique for writing stories – the proverbial 'twist in the tail'.

In *Nomadic Dream*, the lyrics are very straightforward for a male vocalist version, and it is evident that the resolution to the heartache is to walk away and start a new life elsewhere, which, by the lyrics, they do.

In the female vocal version, I have added the words 'Nomadic Dream', after the last line, leaving the listener to contemplate that what the singer really wants – to leave the past behind and start a new life of freedom from the conflict – is, for them, only just a dream and they are stuck in an unhappy situation with no escape. This puts a whole new slant on the emotional effect of the story/song, just by adding two more words, and is a technique that can be used to great effect to make a story/song more memorable.

Finding What to Write About

I once heard a joke that went …

> *I want to be a country singer, but I don't drive a truck, my wife hasn't left me, and my dog hasn't died …*
>
> *(Unknown)*

which I thought was quite hilarious at the time, till I realised that a vast number of 'Country' songs were of that exact or similar vein. Knowing what your theme is, is very important as it will affect the manner in which you tell the story.

Look outside the box for some new and original/possible themes to not fall into same-old, same-old song subjects. And, of course, the best themes are ones that are close to your heart.

We will talk about this more in a later chapter.

2. Imagery

Imagery is another essential technique in lyric writing. Vivid descriptions can transport listeners to specific places and moments, making them feel the emotions being expressed. Here's how to effectively use imagery:

- **Sensory Details**: As in all good story writing, use the five senses – sight, sound, touch, taste, and smell – to bring the scenes (verses) to life. When writing lyrics and poems, you don't have a lot of words to spare to do this as you would in an actual short story when you can add more detail, so you need to rework the original draft to make it the most detailed yet succinct way of describing the story elements. For example, in *Boots for Livin'*, I set the scene and tone of the song with the opening verse:

  Out in the sun where the tall grass sways,
  We gathered 'round on that special day,
  With laughter and stories and a cake homemade,
  For the man we all cherished, every memory played.

  Released in May 2025 on the Album These Country Boots

  This is enough to set the scene and get the story/song rolling.

- **Metaphors and Similes**: These figures of speech create connections between seemingly unrelated ideas, intensifying the emotional resonance.

- A metaphor says something *is* something else, while a simile says it is *'like'* something else. For instance, in my song *Snake in My Life*, the singer continually refers to his/her partner as a snake, with poison in their words and a hiss in their voice, slithering through their life ... The whole song is a metaphor for a vindictive, or selfish, partner and their effect on the singer's life.

- An example of a simile is in the lyrics for Candle in the Night, which says:

'Like a candle in the night, you draw me'.

- **Symbolism**: Use symbolism to represent larger concepts. The singer's love interest in *Snake in My Life* is a perfect example of using a venomous creature to cast turmoil on the singer's partner in life. In my song lyrics *Kiss Away the Rain*, I refer throughout the song to 'the rain in my head ... the rain in my heart ... the rain in my eyes' for the torment and sadness the singer is suffering as she cries in her head, her heart and her eyes as she doubts the loyal intentions of her new lover, and she wants him to kiss away the rain and pledge his love to her.

3. Emotional Expression

At the core of many songs is emotional expression. The ability to articulate feelings through lyrics can create a profound connection with listeners. Without it, the song will be flat, maybe even pointless.

Here are some strategies for emotive writing:

- **Authenticity**: Write what you know, what you've experienced, and what you truly feel. Be true to your feelings. Authenticity resonates deeply with audiences.

For example, in my song lyrics *Cry in My Own Time*, the sadness expressed by the singer which resonates so well with the words written, makes this quite an emotive song. The song was originally written as a poem after a personally devastating experience, being the tragic loss of my dog, my best friend. It was originally titled *Rocky's Song*, the ongoing grief expressed in the lyrics of the fourth verse:

Yet the grief doesn't lessen as days slowly pass
Some days are bad, yet others far worse.
And nobody knows I feel weak and cold
for you were my life, my mate of the soul.

These lyrics could resonate with any listener who has suffered the loss of someone or something dear to them.

- **Vulnerability**: Don't shy away from expressing complex emotions—sadness, joy, fear, longing. Vulnerability can create an intimate bond between the songwriter and the listener.

For example, in the extract from the song lyrics *Bright Star*, on my album *Lyrical Dream*, the truck driver reminisces about his offsider and what life was like with her and now without her, as with the careful selection of words, his grief is laid bare.

I cherish your face in the nighttime
as it shines back to me in the dark
never once had I ever considered
your time on this earth had a mark

With you, Bright Star, up beside me
as the white lines streak on by
the highway was not lonely
and the long miles galloped by

And now these wheels on a highway
moan along this road so far
your face now reflects from the heavens
and you are the brightest star

- **Repetition**: Reiterating certain lines or phrases can emphasise emotions and make them more memorable. A powerful recurring line can encapsulate the song's theme, making it resonate on a deeper level.

For example, the repetition in my song lyrics of *Kimberley Dream*, also on the album *Lyrical Dream*, keeps reiterating all the glorious aspects of the Western Australian northwest region, bringing them to the forefront of the song, as shown in Verse 2 and the Chorus.

White birds overhead that are bickering anew
wing far far away in the Kimberley blue,
to where cockatoos rest in Albizia trees
take my memories soaring on the Kimberley breeze
(Chorus)
of crouched round a fire in a mustering camp
huddling to keep warm in the Kimberley damp;
of lying flat out on a pool crystal deep
soothing the skin in the Kimberley heat.
of droving the cattle across the vast plain
or cleansing the skin in the Kimberley rain
or when stepping to ground from a horse that I trust
to sink my feet deep in the Kimberley dust.

Another example is at the end of a song, where you can re-emphasise the song's main theme, or even change the whole context of the song by changing a few words in the repeated lines.

In *Echoes of the Past*, a song about domestic violence, the last two lines ram the point home of the effect on those who suffered from a brutal husband and father.

(Outro)
As I strum his strings, my eyes still press tight
As my kids sing with me in the evening light
Ma and me should have healed more in time
But the bruises are still in my mind
His bruises still rage in my mind.

The following example shows the plight of a girl following in her father's footsteps, running the farm the way *he* had always run it. She wants him to acknowledge the effort she has made, giving up her life to fulfil his dreams.

(Outro)
So here's my heart and dreams, in every stride I take,
Just a country girl, but I promise I won't break.
I'll keep your legacy alive with every dusty mile,
And maybe one day, Daddy, I pray I'll see you smile.
Then maybe one day, Daddy, you'll make me smile.

Released in May 2025 on the album These Country Boots

Conclusion

Each of these techniques—storytelling, imagery, and emotional expression—can be used individually or in combination to enrich your songwriting. Experimenting with different approaches can help you find your unique voice and style. As you practice, you'll discover that writing lyrics is not just about crafting words, but about weaving together experiences and emotions to create something that resonates with both you and your audience.

Melody Creation:

Crafting Memorable Melodies

Creating a memorable melody is an essential skill for any songwriter or composer. A great melody not only conveys emotion but also captures the listener's attention. Here, we'll briefly explore key elements to consider, including scales, rhythm, and musical hooks.

Understanding Scales: The Foundation of Melody

While not being a musician, I will not go into the construct of each of the scales, and will only mention the effects that each scale type can produce, presuming that if you are reading this section on crafting melodies, you already have a musical background and will understand the various scale types.

For Lyricists, this section might help you instruct your composer/musician on the sort of effect you envisage for your lyrics.

- **Choose the Right Scale**: Begin by selecting a scale that fits the emotional tone of your piece.

- Major scales often evoke feelings of happiness and brightness

- Minor scales can convey sadness or tension, a sombre and often melancholic feel compared to major scales. There are three main types of minor scales: natural minor, harmonic minor, and melodic minor.

- Beyond the major and minor scales are modes such as Dorian, Mixolydian, or Lydian, which have their own character and can inspire fresh melodic lines.

- There is also the Pentatonic Scale, which is a favourite among many musicians due to its simplicity and versatility.

  - Dorian Scale has a slightly jazzy and sophisticated feel to the composition.

  - Mixolydian Scale has a bright sound, often found in rock, blues, and folk music, providing an open and celebratory sound.

  - Lydian Scale has a dreamy and ethereal quality, frequently used in film scores and progressive music.

  - Pentatonic Scale is used for rock, blues, and folk, providing a catchy and harmonious sound.

These scales provide different flavours and emotions, making them essential tools for composers and musicians. Each one can evoke specific feelings or atmospheres, influencing the character of the music in which they are used.

Rhythm: The Heartbeat of Your Melody

- **Syncopation and Offbeats**: Experiment with placing notes on unexpected beats or using syncopation to create interest. This can add a sense of groove and make your melody more engaging. Syncopation and offbeats contribute to the song's rhythmic complexity and appeal.

- **Syncopation** refers to a rhythmic device where the expected rhythmic patterns are disrupted by placing emphasis on beats or parts of beats that are typically weaker or unstressed. This creates a surprising and dynamic effect. For example, in a 4/4-time signature, the strong beats are typically the first and third beats. If you emphasise the second or fourth beat instead, you create syncopation. This unpredictability can add tension and excitement to the music, making it more engaging.

- **Offbeats**, on the other hand, specifically refer to the times between the strong beats in a measure. In a standard 4/4 measure, the offbeats would be the 'ands' between the numbered beats (1-and-2-and-3-and-4-and). These offbeats can also be accentuated to create a lively, driving pulse. Many genres, such as jazz, funk, and reggae, rely heavily on offbeat rhythms to create a distinctive sound.

- Both syncopation and offbeats add rhythmical interest to music, allowing for a more complex and nuanced experience. They are widely used in various genres, contributing to different styles and feels that capture listeners' attention.

- **Vary Note Durations**: Mix long and short notes to create a dynamic rhythmic flow. A melody that alternates between these values can keep the listeners' attention and make certain phrases stand out.

- **Use Repetition Wisely**: Repeating rhythmic patterns can help solidify your melody in the listener's mind. However, be careful not to overuse it – variety is key to maintaining interest. This can include the number of times you include the chorus. Repeating the chorus can encourage the listener to sing-along – if it is repeated too often, it becomes boring.

Crafting Musical Hooks: Your Melody's Signature

Create Contrast: As in writing any novel/story, the beginning must hook the reader (listener) in by piquing their curiosity, or by alerting them with something familiar or intriguing that will excite them enough to keep listening.

One of the best hooks is the introductory melody, guitar riff, or even a drum rhythm to prepare the listener for the start of the vocals. The most memorable songs have a musical introduction that is so unique the listener will immediately know which song is about to play. This hook often showcases a contrast compared to the surrounding material, can be replayed as an instrumental bridge, making the song more memorable and retaining the listener's attention.

Keep It Simple: Many of the most memorable hooks are simple and easy to remember. Aim for clarity over complexity; a hook should be instantly recognisable without being overly intricate.

Emotional Resonance: Ensure your hook resonates emotionally with listeners. Consider the feelings you want to evoke and use melodic intervals and rhythms that align with those emotions. For example, a light, airy tune does not evoke sadness.

Practical Tips for Melody Creation

- **Start with a Motif**: Begin your melody with a small musical idea or motif – one or two bars. From this, you can develop a 'riff' – 4 to 16 bars, then expand on either by altering pitch or rhythm to develop variations of this throughout the song.

- **Sing Your Ideas**: Hum or sing your melodies out loud. This can help you find natural phrasing and flow, allowing you to craft something that feels authentic.

    The lyrics should be spoken, recited, and practised until a natural flow appears, which may or may not require some small edits to correct anything that jars or sounds forced, especially the end rhyme. It is also important to ensure that the rhyming scheme within the song remains consistent, as an inconsistent rhythm can jar. Through repeated verbal treatment of the words, a tune may become apparent that will make the melodic composition easier to achieve.

- **Use Technology**: Take advantage of music production software or apps and devices that offer loop and MIDI (Musical Instrument Digital Interface) functions. A MIDI is a plug and play or Bluetooth piano keyboard that sends sounds to your computer. This can help you experiment and hear your ideas in real-time. If you have the equipment, most certainly record your song, and variations of the song to determine what sounds best. If the combined music and lyrics don't sound like a good fit, try a different music genre. It just might work due to the right emotional slant being capable in some genres and not others.

- **Get Feedback**: Share your melodies with others and gather feedback. Fresh ears can offer new perspectives and suggestions for improvement.

Conclusion

Melody creation is an art that blends techniques, creativity, and emotional expression. Understanding scales, mastering rhythm, and crafting memorable hooks are essential components to producing captivating melodies. With practice and persistence, you can develop the skills needed to create distinctive melodies that resonate with listeners.

If you can master this skill, you jump the fence from lyricist to composer. If you can't master this skill, your musician/composer should become your very best friend.

Finding Inspiration for Songwriting

Songwriting is an intricate art that often requires a burst of inspiration to transform emotions, thoughts, and experiences into lyrics and melodies. Here are some diverse sources from which songwriters can draw their creative sparks:

1. Personal Experiences

One of the most profound wells of inspiration lies within your own life. Drawing from your personal experiences allows you to craft authentic songs that connect with the listener. Whether it's love, heartbreak, joy, or loss, these emotions resonate with listeners because they may have experienced the same situations. Reflect on significant moments—perhaps a cherished memory, a challenging period, or a pivotal life change—and let those stories translate into your songwriting. As they say, 'lay your heart on your sleeve' as in the following lyric examples from *Colour Me Blue* from the *These Country Boots* album:

> (Verse 1)
> *Colour me blue when the skies are grey,*
> *I'm feeling heavy, and lost my way.*
> *My tears shine like the softest rain,*
> *I'm drowning in life's sad refrain.*
> *But deep inside, gold flickers anew,*
> *A glimmer of hope there's life after you.*

(Chorus)
Colour me, oh, colour me blue,
This is the aura when I think of you
Once great elation, now sadness so deep,
This is a colour I don't want to keep.

2. Nature

Nature provides an endless source of inspiration, offering vivid imagery and profound themes. From the gentle rustling of leaves to the awe-inspiring grandeur of mountains, the natural world can evoke deep emotions and reflections. Take long walks, go hiking, or simply sit outside to immerse yourself in your surroundings. Feel the wind in your hair, hear the wind as it whispers past you. It is amazing what your imagination can hear. Write down observations or feelings that arise, focusing on the sights, sounds, and sensations that can transform into metaphor-laden lyrics. The changing seasons, the beauty of a sunset, or even a gentle rain can all spark ideas for songs brimming with emotion, comparisons, and imagery.

For example, in the song lyrics of *Nature's Embrace*, the singer compares a budding romance to the wonder of nature.

(Chorus)
Love's a river flowing, wild and free,
Dancing through the valleys down to the sea.
Mountains high and sturdy, holding dreams so tight,
In every whisper of the wind, our love takes flight.

(Bridge)
Underneath the stars where chandeliers gleam,
We linger together by a babbling stream.
In the moon's silver glow, we're lost to the night,
Guided by our hearts till dawn's early light.

3. Art and Literature

Art in its many forms has the power to ignite creativity. Visual arts, such as paintings and sculptures, can evoke feelings and tell stories that inspire lyrics and tones. Similarly, literature can act as a catalyst; a poignant poem or a compelling novel can lead to new ideas and themes.

I frequently write stories from songs or songs from stories. Sometimes, I need to write a whole story to develop the emotional content of a situation, the personalities of the characters (remember, listeners like songs about people so they can relate to their situations), and finally, to see where the story goes. Remember, songs need a beginning, a middle and an end, or there is no point – it would be like a novel where the last two chapters have been torn out, or a poem that is missing its last verse or punchline. If enough heart tugs and metaphors have appeared in the story, or poem, it becomes a candidate for a musical conversion.

Explore various artistic expressions and consider how they resonate with your own experiences or beliefs. The great advantage of art is its ability to provoke thought and emotion, prompting you to explore those feelings in your songwriting.

4. Current Events

The world is full of stories waiting to be told, and current events provide a rich tapestry of inspiration. Whether it's social movements, political changes, or global challenges, these topics can spark powerful narratives and provoke a strong emotional response. Tap into the mood or atmosphere of a particular period and write songs that reflect the collective consciousness or comment on social issues. This can serve not only as a means of expression but also as a way to connect with listeners who share similar concerns or passions.

My lyrics for *The Trees Bleed* and *Stand Up (for the Earth)* became catchy protest songs when set to vibrant Rock music, which conveys the angst one feels about the destruction of forests or climate change that is being ignored. Songs can really let you get your point across.

Conclusion

Inspiration can come from anywhere, and as a songwriter, remaining open to the world around you is crucial. Personal experiences, nature, art, and current events are just a few of the myriad influences you can draw upon. Engage deeply with each source, allowing them to inform and enrich your songwriting process. Remember, every song has the potential to resonate with others, and your unique perspective can contribute to a collective understanding of our human experience. So grab your pen and let the inspiration flow!

Collaboration in Songwriting

Benefits, Challenges, and Tips for Success

Introduction

Collaborative songwriting is a practice as old as music itself, bringing together diverse ideas, styles, and emotions to create something unique. While it can lead to innovative compositions, co-writing also comes with its own set of challenges. Here, I will explore the benefits of collaboration, the challenges that may arise, and effective strategies to ensure the collaboration process is beneficial.

Benefits of Collaboration

- **Diverse Perspectives:** Collaborating with other musicians allows you to combine different experiences, backgrounds, and musical styles. This diversity can lead to a greater dimension to the compositions, as each songwriter brings their unique experience or slant to the creative process.

    Certainly, a lyricist cannot avoid this collaborative phase of the creative process. You need music – music that matches the mood intended in your lyrics.

- **Idea Sharing and Brainstorming:** Working alongside other creative minds can spark new ideas. The dynamic exchanges that occur in a collaborative environment often leads to unexpected directions that you might not arrive at on your own.

- **Skill Enhancement:** Co-writing exposes musicians to different techniques and practices. By observing and engaging with a partner's writing process, you may discover new tools, methods or music genres to enrich your own songwriting.

- **Increased Productivity:** Having a co-writer can help maintain momentum. The accountability of a partner can inspire consistent output and motivate you to complete projects that might otherwise fade into obscurity, aka the bottom drawer.

- **Networking Opportunities:** Collaborating with other artists can expand your networks and introduce you to new audiences. Each collaboration is an opportunity to tap into the co-writer's fan base, potentially leading to greater exposure and opportunities. This can work both ways. Having a good network within the industry is essential for the word to spread about your talent.

Challenges of Collaboration

- **Creative Differences:** Every songwriter has their own vision and style, which can sometimes clash. Disagreements over lyrics, melody, or arrangement can lead to tension if not managed well.

- **Communication Issues:** Effective communication is vital in any partnership. Misunderstandings and unclear expectations can easily derail the process. It's crucial to establish open lines of communication from the outset.

- **Egos and Ownership:** Some songwriters may feel territorial about their contributions, leading to conflicts over artistic ownership. It's important to navigate these feelings with mutual respect and a clear understanding of roles.

- **Time and Scheduling Conflicts:** Coordinating schedules to ensure both parties can dedicate time to the project can be challenging, especially if collaborators have different commitments. These issues should be discussed before the collaboration begins.

- **Project Direction:** Without a shared vision, collaborators may find themselves pulling in different directions, resulting in a disjointed song. Establishing a common goal is critical for alignment throughout the songwriting process.

Tips for a Fruitful Collaboration

- **Set Clear Goals:** Before beginning the collaboration, discuss your intentions. Are you aiming to write a hit single, an album track, or something experimental? Setting clear objectives can help steer the creative process, particularly in regard to genre and vocalist style.

- **Define Roles:** Establish clear roles for each collaborator. Who will handle lyrics, melodies, instrumentation, or production? Defining responsibilities can minimise conflict and enhance productivity.

- **Foster Open Communication:** Regular check-ins and discussions about the progress can help maintain harmony. Be open to feedback and criticism, as collaboration thrives on trust and honesty.

- **Embrace Flexibility:** While it's essential to have set goals, remaining open to new ideas and directions can lead to unexpected and positive outcomes. Allow the collaboration to evolve naturally, spontaneously, with the understanding that, in this musical journey, you both/all have a piece of the pie.

- **Create a Safe Space for Creativity:** Encourage each other to share ideas without judgment. This supportive atmosphere can help spark inspiration and foster creativity.

- **Establish a Plan for Ownership:** Decide how credits will be assigned for the final piece early on in the process. Will it be equal, or will contributions be weighted differently? Clear agreements can prevent disputes later – that means you should have it in writing so there can be no misunderstandings.

- **Celebrate Small Wins:** Acknowledge progress, whether it's completing a verse or perfecting a chorus. Celebrating achievements can motivate both collaborators and enhance the creative synergy.

Conclusion

Collaboration in songwriting can be a powerful vehicle for creativity, innovation and therefore success. By embracing the benefits, addressing challenges head-on, and applying effective strategies to avoid conflict, songwriters can create a dynamic and rewarding co-writing experience. The mix of ideas and musical styles not only enhances originality, but it can also lead to songs that resonate on a deeper level with listeners. So grab a partner, exchange ideas, and let the magic of collaboration transform your lyrics into music! Because, frankly, words alone do not make a song.

The Importance of Structure in Songwriting

When crafting a song, structure plays a vital role in shaping its overall flow and appeal. A well-defined structure allows listeners to effortlessly engage with the music, enhancing their emotional and visual experience and, therefore, their ability to remember it. Let's explore the common structures found in songs and how they impact their effectiveness.

Common Song Structures

- **Verse-Chorus-Verse (VCV)**

    - This classic structure consists of a verse, followed by a chorus, then another verse, and often returns to the chorus, and so on.

    - The verses typically tell a story or express an emotion, while the chorus serves as the song's emotional centrepiece, delivering a catchy hook. This format creates a rewarding and memorable listening experience, allowing listeners to mentally absorb the narrative while eagerly anticipating the powerful refrain.

A simple example is *Diamonds in the Dust*, an Australian country song that outlines the life of a drover.

Drovers' Day

(Verse)
    Across the wide vast country of mulga, dust and flies
    stockmen build their campfires 'neath diamond-studded skies
    And stretch out on their swag rolls beneath the Boab trees
    To dream about those girls in town
                    while cooled by night's soft breeze.

(Chorus)
    By day, they ride their horses in the dust behind the mob
    Not once ever believing there could be a better job
    For soon a beast will venture to the scrub on either side
    And the stock horse leaps to battle, giving him a thrilling ride.

(Verse)
    The days are long and dusty on a stockhorse taut with pride
    But nowhere would they rather be than on this cattle ride
    The drives that built this nation are remembered far and wide
    From up along the Birdsville Track down to the Great Divide.

(Chorus)
    By day, they ride their horses in the dust behind the mob
    Not once ever believing there could be a better job
    On the drives that built this nation, remembered far and wide
    From up along the Birdsville Track down to the Great Divide

(Verse)
>But then the sun sinks down behind the flat red plain
>And darkness fills the western sky as evening slowly wanes
>The campfire embers filter up from the resting fray
>To join the glittering diamonds at the end of drovers' day.

(Chorus)
>Next day they'll ride their horses in the dust behind the mob
>Knowing deep in their hearts there could be no better job
>And at night again fire embers filter up from the resting fray
>To join the glittering diamonds at the end of drovers' day.

(Outro)
>The drovers' life is diamonds at the end of drovers' day.

Released on the album Lyrical Dreams

- **Verse-Chorus-Bridge (VCB)**

    - Similar to Verse-Chorus-Verse, this structure includes verses and a chorus, but also introduces a bridge – a contrasting section that offers a new perspective or shift in mood.

    - The bridge adds depth to the song by breaking the repetition of verses and choruses. It creates a dynamic turn that can heighten the emotional intensity, giving listeners a refreshing break before returning to the familiar chorus, which may or may not have some slight variation at this point to accommodate the emotional shift in the story.

Country song lyrics work very well with this structure as they tell a story, expand on the story through the chorus, tug at the heartstrings by giving some previously unmentioned details that can change the tone of the story before finalising the song with a conclusion. An example of this is in the lyrics *'In Your Boots'*, from the album *These Country Boots*.

In Your Boots

(Verse 1)
Out in the morning light, with the sun on my face,
I pull on my old boots, meet the day with grace.
I'm out in the fields, the wind ruffling my hair,
Every step I take, Dad, I know you're right there.

(Chorus)
'Cos I'm following your footsteps, every path you've crossed,
In my heart, I carry the lessons, and hope love isn't lost.
Do you see me, Dad, in the way I stand tall?
Working through the seasons ... I'm like you, after all.

(Verse 2)
I hear your laughter in the rustle of the leaves,
Remember how you worked hard, and the dreams you weaved.
You taught me how to cherish every sunrise and dawn,
Now I'm planting my roots here, can you see how far I've come?

(Chorus)
'Cos I'm following your footsteps, every path you've crossed,
In my heart, I carry the lessons, and hope love isn't lost.
Do you see me, Dad, in the way I stand tall?
Working through the seasons ... I'm like you, after all.

(Bridge) ... *This is where the storyline shifts: the character is following in his father's footsteps because he feels guilty that he was not there when his father passed away and he is trying to make amends within himself.*

So here's a little secret, as the stars light the sky,
I'm chasing your dreams, don't you ever wonder why?
I'm sorry I didn't get back before you were gone
With every lonely winding road, I tried to make it back home.

(Chorus)
'Cos I'm following your footsteps, every path you've crossed,
In my heart, I carry the lessons, and pray your love isn't lost.
Do you see me, Dad, in the way I stand tall?
I'm working through the seasons .... I'm like you, after all.

(Outro)
So when the harvest comes, and the sun sets low,
I know you're right beside me, there's so much more to sow.
In your boots, I'm learnin', Dad, with every breeze I chase,
I'm a country boy at heart, and I'm proud to take your place.
I'm a country boy at heart, Dad, and I'm proud to take your place.

The listener is left to ponder whether the Outro is actually the truth.

- **AABA** Structure

    - This format features two similar sections (A), followed by a contrasting section (B), and then returns to the initial section (A).

    - The AABA structure is often used in ballads and jazz songs, but also works well for pop songs, the structure creating a sense of tension and release. The B section serves as a departure from the familiar, leading to a satisfying return that reinforces the song's central theme.

    - An example of this is in the lyrics *Heart of the Night*.

Heart of the Night

(Verse)
*In the heart of the night, where the shadows play,
I wandered alone, lost in my thoughts,
Then a laugh in the dark drifted my way,
A spark of a bond that time slowly caught.*

(Verse)
*You shared all your dreams, your hopes, your delight,
With a smile like the dawn breaking light through the haze,
In a world full of silence, you felt just right,
Together we'd weave our own golden days.*

(Instrumental Bridge)

(Bridge)
> *Through the storms and the calm, hand in hand we stand,*
> *Every secret we share, every moment we roam,*
> *In this journey of life, you're my heart's gentle hand,*
> *With you by my side, I have finally found home.*

(Verse)
> *So let's chase the stars, let our love take flight,*
> *Through the seasons we'll flourish in so many ways,*
> *In the heart of the night, everything feels right,*
> *I know we'll be happy till the end of our days.*

- **Verse-Pre-Chorus-Chorus (VPCC)**

    - In this structure, verses build toward a pre-chorus, which leads directly into the chorus.

    - The pre-chorus acts as a bridge between the narrative of the verse and the emotional highlight of the chorus, intensifying anticipation. This structure is effective in building momentum, leading to a powerful payoff that draws the audience further in.

Waving a Flag

(Verse 1)
> *Late nights alone, silence echoes in the dark,*
> *Empty space in the shadows where we used to park,*
> *You said you needed space, and so I turned away,*
> *But I deeply miss you each and every day.*

(Pre-Chorus)
>We both said things we didn't really mean,
>Now silence fills the air where our laughter had been.
>Fingers crossed behind our backs, we stubbornly wait,
>Caught in the web of love with a pride far too great.

(Chorus)
>If I could just shed my pride,
>And you shed yours tonight,
>We could find our way back home,
>To the place we belong,
>But the walls are high, and the nights feel long.
>Two hearts in a battle, we both feel we're right,
>But let's not war, I'm waving a flag of white.

(Verse 2)
>Scrolling through old photographs, memories flash,
>Every moment sweet, so why did we crash?
>Promises whispered, now they're lost in the air,
>We're two stubborn souls, are we too proud to care?

(Pre-Chorus)
>We tiptoe around our fears, too afraid to fall,
>But deep down, we knew we wanted it all.
>The way we used to laugh, the way we used to dream,
>Now it feels like a distant, even lost, broken theme.

(Chorus)
>If you could just shed your pride,
>And I shed mine tonight,
>We could find our way back home,
>To the place we belong,
>But the walls are high, and the nights feel long.

Two hearts in a battle we don't need to fight,
And so I'm waving a truce flag so white.

(Bridge)
So let's break down these walls we've built,
And wrap each other in love, not guilt.
There's more to say than a heart can hide,
Let's find our way back and throw our pride aside.

(Chorus)
If we could just shed our pride,
Stop ebbing, and roll with the tide,
We could find our way back home,
To the place we belong,
But the walls are high, and the nights feel long.
Two hearts in a battle we don't have to fight,
Love shouldn't be war, let's dance back to the light.

(Outro)
So here's my hand, take it, I'll take yours too,
Let's beat the silence, let's start anew.
In this game of life, let our hearts be our guide,
Let's break the destroying chains of our pride.

- **Chorus-Only Structure**

    - Some songs consist solely of repeated choruses, with minimal or no verses. While less common, this structure can be highly impactful in genres such as pop or electronic music, where a catchy hook is crucial. It allows the song to be immediately recognisable and memorable, and is ideal for dance floors and/or sing-alongs, as in the example *Let's Collide*.

Let's Collide!

(Chorus 1)
>Hey there, strangers, let's collide,
>In this sea of faces, let's take a ride,
>Share a laugh, share a dream,
>In this moment, we're a team!

(Chorus 2)
>Hands together, hearts aligned,
>Every story's waiting, let's unwind,
>New adventures, here we go,
>In this dance, let the magic flow!

(Chorus 3)
>Raise your voice, let it shine,
>In this crowd, we're all divine,
>With every heartbeat, feel the spark,
>In the light, we'll leave our mark!

(Chorus 4)
>Say hello, break down the walls,
>From a whisper to a call,
>Friendship's waiting, take a chance,
>In this moment, come and dance!

A simple song with a regular, repetitive beat that becomes a catchy rhythm to dance to, which is the aim of the song.

The Effect of Structure on Flow and Appeal

The way a song is structured directly influences its flow, that is, the rhythm and pacing of the music. An effective structure creates natural transitions that guide listeners through the song, enhancing its emotional journey.

For example, starting with a softer verse can build anticipation, leading into a powerful chorus that offers a release of energy.

Additionally, the repetition inherent in many song structures contributes to a song's appeal. Catchy choruses invite listeners to sing along, forming a connection between the artist and the audience. By strategically placing memorable hooks and emotionally resonant sections, songwriters can craft an engaging narrative that resonates long after the music has ended.

Conclusion

Understanding and using common song structures is essential for crafting compelling music. By selecting the right structure, songwriters can enhance the emotional impact of their work, capture the listener's attention, and ultimately create songs that resonate with a wide audience. Whether it's through traditional verse-chorus formats or more innovative arrangements, the power of structure is a critical element of writing compelling songs.

Defining Your Style

Finding Your Unique Voice

Every songwriter has a distinct voice that sets them apart from others. Defining your style is an essential step, not only in expressing your creativity but also in connecting with your audience. Here are some strategies to help you discover and enrich your unique sound while drawing from authentic influences.

Self-Reflection: Understand Your Influences

Before diving into songwriting, take time for self-reflection. Consider what inspires you and shapes your musical preferences. Is it the storytelling of folk music, the rhythm of hip-hop, or the melodies of pop?

Make a list of your favourite artists and songs, and dissect what you love about them. Are there common themes or elements of style?

This exploration can guide you toward finding your own voice.

Experiment with Genres

One of the best ways to uncover your unique style is by experimenting across different genres. Write songs in various styles – rock, blues, country, electronic, pop – and notice which elements resonate with you. You might find that blending genres allows you to express your thoughts and emotions more freely. Accept that your style can evolve as you explore new musical styles. And don't be afraid to try a different genre, especially if your lyrics don't work well in the genre you intended them for.

Quite often, I will write country song lyrics, but find they work just as well, or better, in the pop genre. I, therefore, have two options for those lyrics, and can produce two versions, reaching more listeners by catering to their preferences.

Write from Personal Experience

Authenticity stems from genuine expression. Draw upon your personal experiences, thoughts, and feelings when crafting your lyrics. What stories do you want to tell? What emotions do you wish to convey? Using your life as a canvas will not only help you develop a distinctive voice but also create deeper connections with your listeners who may relate to your experiences.

Country music has always been a favourite of mine, and, as the saying goes when writing stories/novels, 'write about what you know', it is just as relevant when writing song lyrics. After numerous trips driving across America, especially through farming areas, I have developed a great respect for the hardworking people who live on the land, and my lyrics often reflect their hardships and family values. I have also had a lifetime of training horses, and this often reflects in my lyrical journey of life as well. Look to what you feel most strongly about to achieve the greatest outpouring of emotion that the listener will relate to.

Develop a Signature Sound

As you explore and experiment, start to identify elements that feel uniquely you. This could be a specific songwriting technique, a favourite chord progression, or even a characteristic vocal delivery. Consistently incorporating these elements will help solidify your identity as a songwriter/lyricist. Consider what sets you apart – is it your lyrical storytelling, your use of metaphor, or the way you blend different styles?

Learn from Influences Without Imitating

Drawing inspiration from other artists is natural, but be careful not to fall into the trap of imitation. Instead, analyse the techniques and styles of your influences and think critically about how they can inform your own craft.

For example, if you admire a particular lyricist, identify what makes their lyrics stand out to you and incorporate similar techniques into your writing while ensuring their essence remains distinctly yours.

Seek Feedback and Collaborate

Sharing your songs with others can offer valuable insights. Join songwriting groups, workshops, or online music communities where you can receive constructive feedback. Collaborating with other musicians can also enhance your songwriting process – different perspectives might inspire unique ideas and help you break out of creative ruts.

Trust Your Instincts

Finally, always trust your instincts. As you navigate the journey of defining your style, you may encounter moments of doubt or comparison to others. Remember that every songwriter has a unique path. Embrace your quirks and idiosyncrasies. Authenticity shines through when you confidently embrace who you are as an artist.

Conclusion

Defining your style as a songwriter or lyricist is not an overnight process – it's a personal journey of exploration, experimentation, and growth – and trial and error. By reflecting on your influences while remaining true to yourself, you can carve out your own niche – your uniqueness. Allow your voice to develop naturally over time, and remember that the most powerful songs often stem from heartfelt expression and authenticity. So grab your instrument, delve into your mind and pen those lyrics, and let your true self resonate through your music.

Using Technology in Songwriting

Modernising the Creative Process

Methods of creating music are constantly changing in this day and age, with technology playing an ever-increasing role in the songwriting process. Today's songwriters have a wide range of tools and software available to streamline and enhance their creative journey – from the initial spark of inspiration to the final product.

Here's how modern technology can aid in songwriting across various stages.

Digital Audio Workstations (DAWs)

At the heart of modern songwriting is the Digital Audio Workstation (DAW), which allows songwriters to compose, record, edit, and mix their music all in one place. Software such as GarageBand, Reaper, Ableton Live, Logic Pro, and Pro Tools are just some of the many platforms that provide interfaces where you can lay down tracks quickly and experiment with different arrangements. With built-in loops and samples, songwriters can jumpstart their compositions and discover new sounds that inspire creativity.

GarageBand and FL Studio are considered good entry-level DAWs, due to their easy-to-use interface, each having its own functionality benefits. Both are considered inexpensive (or free) and are more than suitable for beginner composers, while more serious composers/musicians might prefer to work on professional-level software. Of course, the quality of production and the type of DAW selected will be determined by the capability of the computer it is going to be installed on.

Researching on the internet will help you determine which DAW is the right one for you, and your computer, and MIDI (Musical Instrument Digital Interface) device if you choose to use one.

(If you plan to use virtual instruments in your DAW then a MIDI controller, especially a MIDI keyboard, is a good device to own.)

Here is a short list of possible DAW software to consider. Of course, there are others, but these seem to be the most popular.

- Audacity
- GarageBand.
- FL Studio.
- Reaper.
- Ableton Live.
- Pro Tools.
- Logic Pro
- Cubase.
- Reason.

Recording Technology

Advancements in recording technology have democratised the music-making process. Affordable microphones, audio interfaces, and portable recording devices empower songwriters to capture high-quality audio anywhere. With mobile applications, you can now record ideas or entire tracks on-the-go, ensuring that inspiration is never lost.

3. Songwriting Software and Apps

Dedicated songwriting software, like MasterWriter and Hooktheory, provides invaluable resources specifically designed to assist in the process of creating lyrics and melodies. These platforms offer features such as rhyme dictionaries, thesauruses, and chord progression generators that can help songwriters overcome writer's block.

Collaborative Tools

The rise of cloud-based platforms such as Soundtrap and BandLab has revolutionised collaboration, allowing multiple songwriters to work on the same project from different locations. These platforms feature real-time editing and communication options, making it easy to share ideas, provide feedback, and create a cohesive piece without being face-to-face. This global accessibility fosters creativity and allows for cross-cultural influences to shape songs in remarkable ways.

AI-Powered Tools

Artificial Intelligence is making waves in the music industry, with tools that can suggest chord progressions, generate melodies, or even compose entire tracks. Check out AIVA. Using AI not only provides fresh perspectives and ideas but can also serve as a sounding board for songwriters, pushing them beyond their usual creative boundaries. These technologies learn the user's styles and preferences, offering tailored suggestions that reflect individual uniqueness.

Social Media and Distribution Platforms

Once a song is composed and polished, technology also plays a crucial role in the distribution and promotion of music. Platforms like SoundCloud, Spotify, iTunes, and Bandcamp enable artists to instantly share their work with a global audience. Social media channels enable connections with fans and other artists, creating opportunities for feedback and collaboration. Using these platforms, songwriters can build their brand and foster a supportive community around their music.

Remember, just as in the book publishing business, no book (or song track) sells itself. You need to take advantage of these social media opportunities to market your masterpieces.

Conclusion

Technology has fundamentally reshaped the songwriting process, providing songwriters with tools and resources that enhance creativity and streamline the production process. By embracing these modern solutions – from DAWs and mobile recording to virtual instruments and AI-driven inspiration – songwriters can unlock new dimensions in their music, ensuring their craft continues to evolve with the times. By using the technologies available, songwriters can not only write compelling lyrics and music but also be innovative, collaborative, and share their unique voices with an ever-increasing global music market.

Overcoming Writer's Block

Strategies to Keep the Songwriting Process Flowing

Writer's block can be an insurmountable challenge for songwriters, leaving them feeling frustrated and uninspired. However, there are various strategies you can use to break through these creative barriers and get back to crafting your next hit. Here are several effective methods to overcome writer's block and rejuvenate your songwriting process:

Change Your Environment

Sometimes, a simple change of scenery can stimulate creativity. Try writing in a different location – whether it's a café, park, or even a different room in your home. New surroundings can provide fresh perspectives and inspiration. In a nutshell, get out and feel the world to write about the world.

Set a Routine

Establish a regular songwriting routine to train your brain to be creative at specific times. This can help you enter a creative mindset more easily. Make it a habit to write for a set amount of time each day, regardless of how you feel.

Use Prompts and Challenges

Engage with prompts and challenges to ignite your imagination. This could include writing a song about a specific theme, composing a piece using random words, or participating in songwriting contests. Constraints and deadlines can often lead to innovative ideas.

Team Up with Other Songwriters

Working with other songwriters can often introduce new ideas and perspectives through brainstorming, exchanging lyrics, or co-writing a song. Also, simply engaging in a creative dialogue can help you overcome blocks and inspire new concepts.

Free Writing

Set a timer for 10-15 minutes and write without stopping, editing, or worrying about structure. Allow your thoughts to flow freely, whether they relate to the song you're working on or not. This exercise can help you tap into your subconscious thoughts, often revealing hidden ideas.

Listen to Different Genres

Explore music outside of your usual preferences. Listening to different genres can inspire you with new melodies, rhythms, and lyrical themes. You might discover unique elements that can be adapted into your own songwriting style.

Embrace Imperfection

Give yourself permission to write poorly. Sometimes the pressure to create something perfect can lead to a creative standstill. Accept that your first draft doesn't have to be flawless. Just write and refine later.

Take Breaks

If you feel stuck, step away from your work for a bit. Engage in a different creative activity, such as going for a walk or practising mindfulness techniques. Giving your mind a break can often result in surprising bursts of inspiration when you least expect it – like when you turn the house upside-down looking for a specific item; the moment you stop looking for it, whalla! There it is!

Capture Your Ideas

Always carry a notebook or use a notes app on your phone to jot down random thoughts, lyrics, or melodies as they come to you. This practice can build a reservoir of ideas that you can draw on when you're feeling blocked.

Focus on the Basics

Sometimes it helps to go back to the fundamentals. Work on your melody or chord progressions without worrying about the lyrics. Rebuild your song from the ground up, allowing elements to evolve naturally in a new direction.

Conclusion

Writer's block is a common hurdle for songwriters, but employing a variety of strategies can help you work through it. By changing your environment, fostering collaboration, and embracing imperfection, you can keep your songwriting process flowing. Remember, creativity is a journey, not a destination – allow yourself the space to explore and experiment, and your next brilliant song will be just around the corner.

Analysing Successful Tunes

Grasping the Success Factors

Music is an amazing force that touches people, breaks the barriers of time, language, and culture. However, some tunes reach immense heights of success, reaching the hearts of millions as anthems. To get a better insight into the factors of a song's success, we can dissect hit songs based on lyrics, melody, and emotional appeal.

This is how these factors make a song a success:

Lyrics: The Heart of the Message

- **Relatability and Storytelling**: Great songs usually convey a good story or emotions that one can easily identify with. For example, Adele's *Someone Like You* conveys the pain of a broken heart, using powerful imagery and everyday situations that evoke a strong connection from the listeners. The realism of lyrics resonates deeply, making the song memorable.

- **Hooky Refrains and Choruses**: Most hits have hooks that tend to stick in listeners' heads. For example, Pharrell Williams' *Happy*, with its grating and upbeat chorus, captures the song's topic of happiness. Catchphrases like these encourage sing-alongs and make the song extremely recognisable.

- **Simplicity vs. Complexity**: The interaction between simple and complex lyrics also plays a significant role. Taylor Swift's *Shake It Off* contains simple language and lines that are easy to sing with and understand, while others may have complex metaphors and underlying meanings that resonate with analytical listeners.

2. Melody: The Musical Foundation

- **Trendy Melodic Lines**: A pleasant, memorable melody is a determining factor in the success and enduring power of a song. For instance, the hit *Walk of Life* or *Money for Nothing* by Dire Straits is built upon a hooky guitar riff and sing-along vocal lines, which are immediately recognisable and infectious.

- **Contrasting Sections**: Popular songs use contrasting sections (verses, choruses, bridges) to engage the listeners. The signature 'drop' in Calvin Harris' *Feel So Close* is a strong contrast to the gentle verses, as it presents a rollercoaster of emotions that engages the listeners.

- **Emotional Range**: Melodies have the ability to evoke different emotions through the use of differences in pitch, tempo, and dynamics. Ed Sheeran's *Photograph* harmonises soft verses with heavier acoustic choruses, contributing to the emotional weight of the lyrics. The melodic journey mirrors the rollercoaster nature of the story, resulting in a deep listener experience.

Emotional Impact: Creating Connection

- **Evoking Strong Emotions:** Successful songs often evoke powerful feelings, such as joy, sadness, nostalgia, or empowerment. Billie Eilish's *When the Party's Over* connects on a deeply personal level by using vocal delivery and very little instrumentation to amplify its emotional intensity.

- **Universal Themes:** Songs that tackle universal themes, such as love, loss, and resilience, tend to resonate widely. Consider the worldwide success of *I Will Always Love You* by Dolly Parton and Whitney Houston, which touches on enduring love and farewell, evoking emotions that are universally understood.

- **Cultural Relevance:** The context in which a song is released can also enhance its impact. Songs that resonate with social issues, like Sam Cooke's *Change is Gonna Come*, tackle pressing themes of race and violence, fostering a sense of urgency and relevance that contributes to widespread acclaim.

Conclusion

In summary, analysing successful songs reveals a harmonious blend of relatable and impactful lyrics, unforgettable melodies, and the emotional connections intentionally crafted by the artists. By understanding these elements, songwriters and musicians can structure their craft to create music aimed at resonating deeply with audiences, much like the songs that have become iconic. Whether through storytelling, catchy hooks, or evoking powerful emotions, the magic of music lies in its ability to connect us all.

The Role of Emotion in Songs

Music is a universal language that crosses cultural boundaries, and at the heart of this language lies emotion. The ability to convey strong emotions through lyrics and melodies is what makes a song resonate with listeners and creates lasting connections. In this chapter, I will discuss techniques for conveying emotion in music and why this emotional connection is vital for listeners.

Conveying Strong Emotions Through Lyrics

- **Authenticity and Vulnerability**: Authenticity is key when it comes to songwriting. Listeners are drawn to honesty and vulnerability in lyrics. Sharing personal experiences, struggles, and triumphs allows listeners to feel a genuine connection with the artist. For example, throughout the lyrics of my song *Nature's Embrace*, I use nature and its elements to reveal the love growing between a young couple and how love is so like all facets of nature. The last chorus and Outro wrap up exactly how the singer is feeling.

  (Chorus)
  Love's like a river flowing wild and free
  Dancing through the valleys to the endless sea
  Mountains high and sturdy, holding dreams so tight
  In every whisper of the wind, our love takes flight

(Outro)
So let's paint our love with nature's embrace
In every facet, together we'll trace
From the sunrise to the stars, let the whole world know
In the heart of nature, our love will always glow
And I let the whole world know ... I love you so ...

- **Imagery and Metaphor**: Effective use of imagery and metaphor can evoke strong emotions by painting vivid pictures in the listener's mind. Instead of stating feelings outright, metaphors can deepen the meaning and stir emotions. For instance, comparing love to a wildflower or heartbreak to a storm can create a more impactful experience. An example of this is in the lyrics of *Candle in the Night*, where the singer is coming out the other side of the despair of a broken relationship.

  Like a candle in the darkest night
  You draw me
  You fill my darkest hour with light
  So I can see
  You're the calming of my storm-tossed sea
  Soothe my turbid heart
  You repaired my tattered sails so I'm sailing free

  Dark oceans far apart
  With candles' warmth, dark memories depart
  My angel of the night
  You spread your wings around my heart
  And now I've taken flight
  Love's angel ...

- **Use of Language and Sound**: The choice of words and the sound of the lyrics contribute to the emotional weight of a song. Poetic devices – such as alliteration, assonance, and rhythm – can enhance thematic depth and emotional resonance. Incorporating contrasting emotions within a song can also create tension, leading to a more powerful payoff when the emotional climax is reached.

As an example, I have inserted the whole of the lyrics of *Embers and Blue* to demonstrate the shifting emotions within the whole song and how the stockman's situation with his companions has now been reversed.

Embers and Blue

The campfire glowed red 'gainst the backdrop of night,
the sky was peppered with stars,
'neath a tree on the plain a stockman reclined,
on his jew-harp he strummed a few bars.

And he stared at the embers, his mind far away,
his aloneness irking him not,
for the dog at his feet and the horse he'd turned out
was all that a man could want.

His life as a Drover had been fairly good,
though he'd seen his fair share of bad too,
but ne'er did he grieve while his mates were afoot,
Old Plodder and dog, Jimmy Blue.

And he wondered now as he stared at the flames
as the dog rose and came to his side,
what else to do now that age was about
and he was no longer able to ride?

And what of the dog, his best friend in life,
– he'd had others – Mate, Harry and Jack -
and he remembered the pain as he'd buried each one
way out there on the overland track.

And he thought of the tears that still welled as he passed
the markers where each one now lay,
and he stroked the pup's brow and forced back the thought
that Blue, too, would be out there one day.

But the flickering flames fired other thoughts up,
a ponderance of what was ahead.
What would Blue do when it happened to pass
that he was the first to be dead?

Would Blue stay by his side, and cry at the find,
if his life passed away with the night?
Would he sit through the dark and reflect on the times
they had had till the grey early light?

And what if he did, (as he'd done in the past),
would he stay till his life too was done?
Or else pad the trails they had travelled for years,
for life forever moves on.

And staring now into Blue's worried eyes,
he stroked his best pal with old hands,
and rued the thought of him dying alone,
unable to live off the land.

Or maybe he prayed, wheezing out life's last tune,
he'd join with a dingo mob ...
then in sounds of the night, his eyes rolled to the sky –
He left it all up to God.
He left it all up to God.

This song is a straight through Verse-Verse-Verse, with no chorus or bridge to break up or distract the flow of the story. The alliteration of *'flickering flames fired' other thoughts up'* shifts the man's thoughts of dying and the loss of his previous dog-companions to the fact that now the situation was the dog, his best friend, being left behind with *his* passing.

Conveying Strong Emotions Through Music

- **Melody and Harmony**: The melody is often the most memorable part of a song and can evoke specific emotions through its shape and progression. Minor keys generally evoke sadness or melancholy, while major keys tend to convey happiness and brightness. Additionally, the arrangement of chords can amplify the emotional tone; **dissonance** (when two or more tones clash and create a harsh, unpleasant sound) can create tension, while **consonance** (when two or more tones complement each other to produce a sound that is pleasant to the ear) can provide resolution and comfort.

- **Dynamics and Tempo**: The dynamic range of a song – the variations in volume – can heighten emotional responses. Soft, quiet passages often evoke intimacy or vulnerability, while loud, powerful sections can generate excitement or urgency. Similarly, tempo can greatly influence emotion: a slow tempo may induce introspection, while an upbeat tempo can inspire joy and energy.

When writing lyrics, it is a good idea to try different tempos, ranges and genres to see what gives the most emotional impact to the theme you are creating.

- **Instrumentation and Production**: Different instruments inherently carry emotional tones. String instruments, such as violins and cellos, often communicate sorrow and depth, while brass can convey strength and boldness. The production techniques, such as **reverb** – which is when a sound occurs in a space, sending out sound waves in all directions, which then bounces off surfaces in that space and eventually diminish to nothing – and **layering** – which is when you use your digital audio workstation (DAW) to combine multiple sounds, such as melodies, riffs, or chords etc., into a richer, more complex sound – can enhance the emotional depth of the song and thereby invoke the emotions of the listener. So experiment with the various instruments to find which ones best create the intention of the song lyrics.

The Vital Connection for Listeners

This connection between emotion in music and the listener is fundamental for several reasons:

- **Relatability**: When listeners hear a song that expresses emotions they feel but may struggle to articulate, they find comfort in knowing they're not alone. Music can provide a powerful cathartic reflection of personal experiences, giving solace and validation to the listener.

- **Therapeutic Effects**: Many listeners turn to music as a form of therapy. The emotional content of a song can evoke memories, help process grief, or provide a means of escapism. Music can act as a cathartic release or a guide through difficult emotions, ultimately aiding mental health and well-being.

- **Community and Connection**: Songs often become anthems that foster a sense of community among listeners, creating shared experiences that bring people together. Celebrating joy, mourning loss, or navigating life's complexities through song provides a sense of belonging and collective understanding.

You only have to think of singing in a church or sitting around the campfire singing *Kumbaya*.

Conclusion

In summary, the role of emotion in songs is pivotal in creating a profound connection between the music and its listeners. By employing lyrical authenticity, compelling imagery, dynamic melodies, and thoughtful instrumentation, songwriters can craft powerful emotional experiences. This is just as important an aspect for the lyricist to consider as it is for the composer. For listeners, the emotional journey weaves through memories, offering comfort and fostering connection, making music an essential and cherished aspect of human life.

Performing Your Songs

Transitioning from Writing to Stage

Transitioning from writing songs to performing them live can be an exhilarating yet terrifying experience. While writing allows for introspection and personal expression, performing requires a totally different set of skills, primarily focused on engaging with an audience and building connections. Here's a guide to help you navigate this important step in your musical journey, if you choose to take it rather than employ seasoned performers.

Understanding the Shift

- From Personal to Universal: When you write a song, it often comes from a deeply personal place. However, performing it live means sharing that personal experience with an audience who may not share the same background or emotions. The challenge is to transform your individual feelings into a universal experience that resonates with listeners.

- **Crafting a Narrative:** Consider each performance an opportunity to tell a story. Think about the emotions behind your song and how you can convey them through your performance. Providing a contextual narrative, like a brief backstory about the song, can help the audience connect more deeply.

Engaging Your Audience

- **Make Eye Contact:** One of the simplest yet most effective ways to engage your audience is through eye contact. Scanning the room and locking eyes with individual audience members can create a sense of intimacy, making them feel included in your performance. Your performance, by the way, is all about **them**, not you.

- **Use Body Language:** Your body language communicates a wealth of information, sometimes even more than your words. Move with purpose, use gestures to emphasise moments in your song, and be aware of your posture. A confident performer draws the audience in. Don't just sing the words – sing the emotion!

- **Involve the Audience:** Encourage audience participation by getting them to sing along, clap, or even dance, if the song is suitable for this. This invites them to share their experiences related to your song's message. This can create a lively atmosphere and make your performance more memorable.

Building a Connection

- **Be Authentic:** Authenticity is key to connecting with your audience. Share your true self, including your vulnerabilities and passions. Don't be afraid to show emotion during your performance; it makes your connection with the audience more genuine.

- **Read the Room:** Pay attention to the audience's reaction. If they seem engaged, continue with your current energy and momentum. If not, don't hesitate to adapt your approach—perhaps by changing your setlist or interacting more directly.

- **Practice Storytelling:** Storytelling can transform a performance. Including anecdotes or moments of reflection builds rapport with your audience. For example, sharing a personal struggle related to a song can cultivate empathy and understanding. Performers who simply sing one song after another with no interaction with the audience often appear like they really don't want to be there. Connect through dialogue, not just song lyrics.

Preparing for Performance

- **Practice, Practice, Practice:** Perfect your songs before you hit the stage. Familiarise yourself with both the music and the lyrics, so you can focus on your performance rather than worrying about mistakes. Video record your performance or, at the very least, tape your voice performance so you can watch and listen to how well you performed. This is a great confidence booster when you realise you have performed and sounded well.

- **Simulate the Experience:** Rehearse in front of friends or family to simulate the live performance experience. Dress appropriately for the style of music – if you sing 'country', look 'country'. Even buy a hat! If you sing pop, dress casual; if you rap, wear gold chains and a hoodie – just kidding. The best advice I can give is to study what to top names in the genre are wearing and dress similarly. Whatever you wear, look professional to keep your credibility.

- After your trial performance, ask for feedback on your stage presence and engagement, and make adjustments based on your audience's reactions.

- **Consider the Venue:** Each venue has its own unique atmosphere, acoustics, and audience. Tailor your performance to fit the environment – sometimes a softer, more acoustic version of a song works better in an intimate setting, while a lively rendition might be ideal for larger crowds in an auditorium.

Handle Performance Anxiety

- **Embrace the Nerves:** Feeling nervous before a performance is entirely normal. Instead of fighting it, embrace the adrenaline. It can enhance your performance and connect you with the audience, as your vulnerability may resonate with them.

- If you have 'practised, practised, practised', and filmed yourself, and recorded your voice, and considered you are really ready for a real live audience, visualise yourself in your mind's eye doing that performance. This goes a long way to reducing the nerves. Visualise it during the day; visualise it just before you go to sleep at night, and visualise it in the quiet moments before you go on. Do this and you will feel, when you step on that stage, that you have performed numerous times before.

- **Breathe and Centre Yourself:** Before taking the stage, practice breathing techniques to calm your nerves. Grounding yourself can help you centre your focus and better connect with the audience.

Conclusion

The journey from writing songs to performing them can feel like a leap of faith, but with practice, authenticity, and audience engagement, it can be one of the most rewarding aspects of being a musician. Embrace the opportunity to share your art, connect with others, and allow your songs to come alive on stage. By fostering a genuine relationship with your audience, you not only elevate your performance but also create a memorable experience for both yourself and your listeners.

Self-Publishing and Promotion for Songwriters

In the digital age, self-publishing has emerged as a viable path for songwriters wishing to share their music with the world. With the right strategies, independent musicians can not only release their songs, but also effectively market them to reach a wider audience. Here are some insights and tips for songwriters on self-publishing and promoting their work:

Understanding Self-Publishing

Self-publishing gives songwriters full control over their music, including how it is produced, distributed, and marketed. It allows for creative freedom and the opportunity to directly connect with listeners. Here are some key components:

- **Distribution Services:** Use platforms like DistroKid, Tunecore, or CD Baby to get your music on major streaming services (Spotify, Apple Music, Amazon Music) and digital storefronts (iTunes, Google Play).

    There are numerous other platforms but, with all of them, check out how much they pay per stream, whether they claim ownership of your music, or a share of it, and whether they charge a fee and/or have limits on how many tracks you can upload.

- **Licensing and Royalties:** Understand the importance of registering your songs with performance rights organisations (PROs) such as ASCAP, BMI, or SESAC to collect royalties from public performances and radio plays.

Creating High-Quality Recordings

Before releasing your music, invest in high-quality recordings. This doesn't necessarily mean heading to a high-end studio. With the right equipment and software, you can produce professional-sounding tracks at home. Consider:

- **Recording Software:** Get familiar with Digital Audio Workstations (DAWs) like Logic Pro, Ableton Live, or GarageBand.

- **Production Quality:** Pay attention to mixing and mastering, or consider hiring a professional for these crucial final steps.

Building Your Brand

Your brand as a songwriter is integral to your success. Consider the following:

- **Visual Identity:** Develop consistent branding across your social media platforms, website, and promotional materials through logos, colours, and imagery.

- **Artist Biography:** Write a compelling artist bio that tells your story, influences, and what makes your music unique. This will resonate with your audience and the press.

Digital Marketing Strategies

Once your music is ready, using digital marketing platforms is the key to success. Here are effective strategies:

- **Social Media Presence:** Use platforms like Instagram, TikTok, Facebook, and Twitter to connect with fans. Share behind-the-scenes content, music teasers, and engage with followers regularly.

- **Email Marketing:** Build an email list to keep fans updated on new releases, shows, and exclusive content. Services like Mailchimp or Substack can streamline this process.

- **Content Creation:** Start a blog or vlog that provides insights into your songwriting process, musical influences, or offers tips for other songwriters.

5. Networking and Collaborations

Collaborating with other artists can expose your music to new audiences. Attend local music events, workshops, and online forums to connect with fellow musicians.

- **Join Songwriter Groups:** Look for local or online songwriter collectives where you can collaborate, share feedback, and perform together.

- **Seek Opportunities:** Network with producers, musicians, and influencers who might help promote your music. Watch for collaboration opportunities with content creators who already have a following.

Live Performances

Performing live is an effective way to promote your music:

- **Local Venues:** Start with open mic nights or gigs at local bars and cafes. This can help you build a local fan base.

- **Livestream Concerts:** Use platforms like Instagram Live, Facebook Live, or YouTube for virtual performances, which can reach a global audience.

Music Videos and Visual Content

Creating music videos or visualisers can significantly boost your online presence. Even simple video productions can increase engagement and provide visual appeal on social media platforms.

Use Music Promotion Services

Consider using music promotion services to help get your music in front of the right audiences. Services like SubmitHub enable you to send your music to bloggers, playlist curators, and radio stations.

Conclusion

Self-publishing and promoting your music as a songwriter enables you to share your talent and stay abreast of changes within the music industry. By equipping yourself with the right tools, embracing digital marketing, and engaging with your audience authentically, you can successfully gain a following that will hold you in good stead in this vibrant world of music. Remember, persistence and passion are key. Keep writing, sharing, and connecting – and your next single could bring new listeners to your previous tracks.

Songwriting Challenges

Lyric writing challenges can be an effective way to ignite creativity and refine your writing skills. Here are some creative prompts and challenges you can try to embrace and enhance your lyric-writing abilities.

I keep a jar, called The Creative Cauldron, which holds a variety of prompts and topics, gathered from numerous random sources, that I draw from to poke my imagination.

Below is a sampling of similar exercises from the Creative Cauldron.

Random Word Challenge

- **Prompt:** To expand your vocabulary and encourage thinking outside the box, pick five random words from a dictionary or word generator. Write a song that incorporates all five words in a meaningful way.

Genre Switch-Up

- **Prompt:** Explore different musical styles and adapt your writing accordingly by taking a well-known song and rewriting it in a different genre (e.g. convert a pop song into a country ballad).

Emotional Rollercoaster

- **Prompt:** To foster emotional depth and narrative complexity in songwriting, write a song that tells a story exploring a range of emotions – joy, sadness, anger, and hope. Try to transition smoothly between each emotion.

Imagery Exploration

- **Prompt:** To hone your descriptive skills and enhance lyrical imagery, write a song solely based on imagery from a specific setting (e.g., a bustling city street, a tranquil forest, a raging ocean). Use sensory details to create vivid pictures, then insert your character/s into the scene.

First Line Inspiration

- **Prompt:** Learn to develop ideas from a singular starting point by using a random first line generated from a book or text. Build a song around it, creating a narrative that flows from that opening.

Collaboration Challenge

- **Prompt:** To foster teamwork, pair up with another participant, but instead of co-writing a full song, each person contributes a verse, chorus, or bridge without revealing their part until it's combined. Decide on the song theme before commencing.

Three-Minute Songwriting

- **Prompt:** To develop spontaneity and free-flow writing, set a timer for three minutes and write as many lines as possible in that time. After the time is up, choose the best lines or rearrange the lines to form a cohesive song.

Perspective Shift

- **Prompt:** To stimulate fresh ideas, write a song from a unique perspective or from another character's point of view from a song you have already written. There are usually two sides to a story, especially with songs about relationships. You could even take the viewpoint of an inanimate object, an animal, or even a bystander.

Syllable Structure

- **Prompt:** To improve rhythm and poetic structure, write a song where each line has a specific syllable count (e.g., 7-5-7-5 pattern). Maintain a coherent theme throughout.

Memory Lane

- **Prompt:** To develop the skill of introspection and personal storytelling in lyrics, write a song based on a specific childhood memory or a significant moment in your past, capturing the feelings and details associated with it.

The Colour Challenge

- **Prompt:** To develop synesthesia, choose a colour and write a song that embodies the feelings, moods, and imagery associated with it, without stating the colour. This can bring powerful emotional and visual imagery to the lyrics. (Synesthesia occurs when words or images you create evoke a particular colour in the listener's mind.)

Mash-Up Madness

- **Prompt:** Push your creativity by selecting two totally unrelated songs and combining their themes, melodies, or lyrics to create a new piece.

You can either complete these challenges individually or work with a partner, sharing your creations at the end of the session for constructive feedback. By regularly engaging in these prompts and challenges, you can develop your skills, broaden your musical horizons, and ultimately find your unique voice.

Emotion Exploration

- **Prompt**: Write a song that captures a specific emotion (e.g., joy, sadness, anger, nostalgia) without explicitly stating it. Use metaphors and imagery to convey the feeling.

Storytelling in Verse

- **Prompt**: Write a song that tells a story with a clear beginning, middle, and end. Use five specific events or moments that create a narrative arc.

Object Inspiration

- **Challenge**: Select an everyday object (e.g., a coffee cup, an umbrella, a bicycle) and write a song that personifies this object, exploring its experiences and emotions.

Setting the Scene

- **Challenge**: Write a song that paints a vivid picture of a specific location (e.g., a beach at sunset, a bustling city street, or a quiet forest). Focus on sensory details – sight, sound, taste, touch and smell – to immerse the listener in the setting.

Character Study

- **Prompt**: Create a song from the perspective of a fictional character (a superhero, a villain, a historical figure), or even a person you have met, exploring their thoughts and feelings in a pivotal moment in their story.

Musical Haiku

- **Challenge**: Write a haiku (three lines with a 5-7-5 syllable structure) and then expand it into a full song. Use the essence of the haiku to inspire the verses and chorus.

First Line Hook

- **Prompt**: Start with a powerful first line that captures attention. Build an entire song around this line, ensuring it reappears within the chorus.

Influence and Inspiration

- **Challenge**: Choose a natural element (e.g. wind, rain, sun) and write a song inspired by it. Examine how it influences human emotions, relationships, and life experiences.

Dialogue and Interaction

- **Prompt**: Write a song as a conversation between two characters. Capture their dialogue in lyrics, focusing on their differing perspectives or voices.

One Word Wonder

- **Challenge**: Choose a single word (e.g., 'freedom', 'time', 'heart', for example) and create a song that explores various themes and ideas linked to that word. Aim for depth and complexity in the lyrics.

Musical Picture Album

- **Prompt**: Create a series of short songs (1 to 2 minutes each) that each depict a different 'picture' or scene from your life. Treat each song like a snapshot, focusing on vivid imagery.

The 10-Minute Song

- **Challenge**: Set a timer for 10 minutes and write as much of a song as you can in that time. Focus on spontaneous creativity without overthinking or editing your ideas.

Last Line First

- **Prompt**: Begin with the last line of a song and write the verses and chorus that lead into it. Build the narrative or theme backward from that concluding thought.

Each of these challenges encourages you to think outside the box, experiment with different styles, and enhance your songwriting skills. Share your creations with your collaboration partner or group for constructive feedback and inspiration.

Happy writing!

Building a Songwriting Community

The Value of Networking with Other Songwriters

Songwriting can often feel like a solitary pursuit, but the truth is that the best songs often come from collaboration, feedback, and shared experiences. One of the most powerful assets a songwriter can have is a strong community of fellow musicians. Here's why building a songwriting community is invaluable to you and how to effectively engage with it.

- **Collaborative Inspiration:** Surrounding yourself with other songwriters exposes you to diverse perspectives and styles. Whether it's a catchy melody, a unique lyrical approach, or fresh songwriting techniques, your peers can inspire you in ways you might not have thought possible. A simple jam session can lead to a powerful co-written song or the spark for your next big idea.

- **Constructive Feedback:** Sharing your work with trusted peers can provide invaluable insights. Honest critiques can help you hone your skills, whether it involves tightening up a lyric, adjusting the arrangement, or suggesting an entirely new direction for a song. Constructive feedback and/or compliments can elevate your work and give you the confidence to take risks.

- **Accountability:** Being part of a songwriting community can keep you motivated and accountable. When you know you have a group of peers waiting to hear your latest drafts or song ideas, you're more likely to dedicate time to your craft. This accountability can be especially beneficial during periods of self-doubt or creative black holes.

- **Shared Resources:** A songwriting network can provide access to shared resources, such as industry contacts, performance opportunities, and writing prompts. Your peers may have the connections to open doors of opportunity that might not be accessible to you as a solo, isolated artist. You can also learn about local open mics, contests, and workshops through your peers' and/or their connections.

Participating in Workshops and Songwriting Groups

- **Skill Development:** Workshops are structured environments where you can actively learn from experienced songwriters and industry professionals. These settings provide opportunities to explore new techniques, receive specialised feedback, stay up-to-date with trends, and develop your skills in a supportive atmosphere.

- **Networking Opportunities:** Workshops and songwriting groups are perfect places to meet other musicians. You may discover a collaborator for your next project or a mentor who can guide you through the industry's intricacies. Building relationships in these settings can lead to future opportunities and support.

- **Community Support:** Being part of a group can combat the isolation many songwriters experience. Regular interaction with fellow musicians creates a sense of belonging and shared purpose. Sharing in each other's highs and lows fosters a supportive environment that encourages growth and creativity.

- **Diverse Experiences:** Joining a songwriting group or groups can expose you to a wide range of genres and styles, which can broaden your musical scope by introducing you to new styles and techniques.

How to Get Started

- **Join Local Groups:** Look for local songwriting groups or workshops in your community. Many local music schools, community centres, and art organisations offer songwriting courses and meetups.

- **Use Online Platforms:** If you can't find local resources, explore online songwriting communities. Platforms such as Reddit, Facebook groups, or dedicated songwriting forums can provide a wealth of information and opportunities to connect with other songwriters.

- **Attend Music Festivals:** Many music festivals offer songwriting workshops and networking events. Attend these to learn and to connect with other songwriters and industry professionals.

- **Create Your Own Group:** If you're struggling to find an existing community, consider forming your own. Reach out to fellow musicians and set regular meetings to share your work and exchange ideas.

Conclusion

Building a songwriting community isn't just about networking; it's about finding inspiration, developing your craft, and creating lasting relationships with fellow musicians. By actively participating in workshops and engaging with other songwriters, you'll not only enhance your skills but also create a supportive environment that nurtures your creativity and artistic growth. Take the plunge – connect, collaborate, and watch your songwriting flourish!

Examples of Lyrical Inspiration

In previous chapters, I have shared some of the lyrics of my songs to demonstrate the point I was trying to make.

I am a firm believer that when learning a new skill, 'if I hear, I will forget; if I see, I will remember; if I do it, I will understand'.

New skills are generally best retained with a hands-on approach. While I cannot conduct physical activities with you in this book, I can at least show you the process I take and explain the inspiration and how I achieved the final lyrics in some of my songs, in the hope you will gain some insight into some of the processes that will help to spark your creativity.

Some of the lyrics I use in this section are converted from poems I had written many years ago that were considered (pretty much) a defunct style in the current poetic trend. Rhyming poets, take heart! There is still a place for our creative genius!

When creating the lyrics, I could hear the music in the words, and knew the genre the song-story was targeted at. It was then a matter of collaborating with composers/musicians with a clear intent of what I was aiming for. Being open to suggestions, tweaking words here and there to add more depth or dimension, and possibly changing the genre of some of them has proved immensely beneficial. Be creative, but also be open to improvement. As Creatives, we can be rather protective of our creations, which can at times be to our detriment as artists.

Lyrics and Process

Candle in the Night was originally written as an example of an old French form of poetry called a Virelay in my book *Everything You Need to Know About ... Writing Poetry – Simplified*. It's original title was *Love's Angel*. Below is the original poem.

Love's Angel

>Like a candle in the darkest night
>You draw me
>You fill my darkest hour with light
>So I can see
>You're the calming of my storm-tossed sea
>Soothe my turbid heart
>You repaired my tattered sails so I'm sailing free
>Dark oceans far apart
>With candles' warmth, dark memories depart
>My angel of the night
>You spread your wings around my heart
>And now I've taken flight.

Without adding any new content and incorporating the title throughout the lyrics, I simply split the poem into two verses, then repeated existing lines in different places to lengthen it to a song. With the addition of piano and emotive vocals, whalla! – a new song was born.

Candle in the Night

Like a candle in the darkest night
You draw me
You fill my darkest hour with light
So I can see
You're the calming of my storm-tossed sea
Soothe my turbid heart
You repaired my tattered sails so I'm sailing free

Dark oceans far apart
With candles' warmth dark memories depart
My angel of the night
You spread your wings around my heart
And now I've taken flight

Love's Angel
You fill my darkest hour with light
Soothe my turbid heart
You spread your wings around my soul
And now I've taken flight

Love's Angel
Like a candle in the darkest night
You draw me
and spread your wings around my soul
And now I've taken flight

Kimberley Dream

The inspiration behind *Kimberley Dream* came while camping on an outback station during a training exercise in the Kimberley region of the most beautiful northwest of Western Australia. With intense heat burning our skin during the day, warranting a swim in the Wununurra Gorge, and an intense storm building across the landscape at night, I lay in my swag watching the lightning strikes getting closer and closer as this poem formed in my head and was complete by morning.

Converting it to song lyrics simply required selecting suitable verses for the Chorus and the Bridge, as outlined by italics in the song lyrics.

Kimberley Dream (poem)

To wake in my swag with a wide stretching yawn
and be gently caressed by a Kimberley dawn
in a camp that I pitched by a cold rippled stream
is only a part of my Kimberley dream.

White birds overhead that are bickering anew
wing far far away in the Kimberley blue,
to where cockatoos rest in Albizia trees
take my memories soaring on the Kimberley breeze

of crouched round a fire in a mustering camp
huddling to keep warm in the Kimberley damp;
of lying flat out on a pool crystal deep
soothing the skin in the Kimberley heat.
of droving the cattle across the vast plain

or cleansing the skin in the Kimberley rain
or when stepping to ground from a horse that I trust
to sink my feet deep in the Kimberley dust.

When I left this land long time my heart sorely hurt
till I lay my swag back in the Kimberley dirt
In the Kimberley sun or the Kimberley flood
the life in this land is my Kimberley blood.
And now in my swag watching black clouds form
I know it's the first of the Kimberley storms

The changes are coming, no seasonal regret
It's time for the winter - the Kimberley wet
When rainfall eradicates land's steamy haze
giving relief from hot Kimberley days
where far and wide such magnificence seen
rolls on and on in new Kimberley green.

After droving long years in this glorious land
I'll give my bones up to the Kimberley sand
To die in the top-end's a sure-fired must
so my soul can drift on in the Kimberley dust

And now that I've lived to life's journey's end
I let my soul fly on the Kimberley wind
I lie on my swag as life passes me by
'neath a boab tree 'neath a star-filled Kimberley sky

Kimberley Dream (song)

To wake in my swag with a wide stretching yawn
and be gently caressed by a Kimberley dawn
in a camp that I pitched by a cold rippled stream
is only a part of my Kimberley dream.

White birds overhead that are bickering anew
wing far far away in the Kimberley blue,
to where cockatoos rest in Albizia trees
take my memories soaring on the Kimberley breeze

of crouched round a fire in a mustering camp
huddling to keep warm in the Kimberley damp;
of lying flat out on a pool crystal deep
soothing the skin in the Kimberley heat.
of droving the cattle across the vast plain
or cleansing the skin in the Kimberley rain
or when stepping to ground from a horse that I trust
to sink my feet deep in the Kimberley dust.

When I left this land long time my heart sorely hurt
till I lay my swag back in the Kimberley dirt
In the Kimberley sun or the Kimberley flood
the life in this land is my Kimberley blood.
And now in my swag watching black clouds form
I know it's the first of the Kimberley storms

The changes are coming, no seasonal regret
It's time for the winter - the Kimberley wet

When rainfall eradicates land's steamy haze
giving relief from hot Kimberley days
where far and wide such magnificence seen
rolls on and on in new Kimberley green.

of crouched round a fire in a mustering camp
huddling to keep warm in the Kimberley damp;
of lying flat out on a pool crystal deep
soothing the skin in the Kimberley heat.
of droving the cattle across the vast plain
or cleansing the skin in the Kimberley rain
or when stepping to ground from a horse that I trust
to sink my feet deep in the Kimberley dust.

After droving long years in this glorious land
I'll give my bones up to the Kimberley sand
To die in the top-end's a sure-fired must
so my soul can drift on in the Kimberley dust

And now that I've lived to life's journey's end
I let my soul fly on the Kimberley wind
I lie on my swag as life passes me by
'neath a boab tree 'neath a star-filled Kimberley sky

So, they are a couple of examples of how it is possible to convert poems into song lyrics simply by playing with the location and repetition of lines to make a greater impact.

I will now provide some examples of how to gain fresh ideas when you have a creative block, and how I used this method to write *Snake in My Life*.

After overhearing a conversation and picking up on the metaphor 'snake in the grass', I decided to play with the metaphor and see what eventuated.

First, I gave myself five minutes to make a list of all the things I could think of relating to snakes, and came up with the following:

Lurk in the shadows, slither; sounds like a whisper when they slither through the grass, venom, poisonous, hissing sound, bite, in the grass, coil up, shed their skin, go around them, look like they are smiling, cold-blooded, stay out of their way!

The metaphor 'snake in the grass' refers to a treacherous person, so I put my list of snake words together and related them to a person and how they would affect another person, such as a romantic interest. What resulted from playing with the words and lines, the melody and tempo, without changing the lyrics I produced a version in the pop genre and also a version suitable as a Country song. Being careful with the wording to keep the lyrics universal, the song can be sung by male or female vocalists, thereby producing two versions of the same song.

Note the extra emotive impact in the very last line where the singer states 'the world is my playground', indicating they intend to head as far away from the 'snake' as they can possibly get.

Here are the final lyrics.

Snake in My Life

(Verse 1)
In the shadows, I can see you crawl,
A silken whisper, tempting me to fall.
Coiled around my dreams, you weave your lies,
But your charming smile is a thin disguise.

(Chorus)
You're the snake in my life, shedding my light,
Carrying my dreams away, hiding in the night.
With poison in your words and a hiss in your voice,
It's time to break free, I have the choice.

(Verse 2)
You slither through my thoughts, sweet but cold,
Every touch a promise, your heart without soul.
Venom drips from fingers that once held me tight,
Now I see the truth and rise up against you and fight.

(Chorus)
You're the snake in my life, shedding my light,
Carrying my dreams away, hiding in the night.
With poison in your words and a hiss in your voice,
It's time to break free, I have the choice.

(Bridge)
I won't let you coil around my heart,
I'll cut the ties, make a brand new start.
Leave the snake behind, you're a snake in the grass,
I'll reclaim my joy and won't let this moment pass.

(Chorus)
You're the snake in my life, shedding my light,
Carrying my dreams away, hiding in the night.
With poison in your words and a hiss in your voice,
It's time to break free, I have the choice.

(Outro)
So I'll rise from your shadow, leave you in the past,
No more tangled dreams, my freedom will last.
A life without venom, a new life I'll find,
Stepping into the sunlight, I leave the snake behind.
The world is my playground and I leave the snake behind.

***

As a lyricist and/or songwriter, one of the tools of the trade is to 'people watch'. So many stories can be imagined by watching people and putting your own determination into what is going on.

I was at a party once and was intrigued by a young couple who had obviously had an argument prior to arriving. While she sat, seemingly having a good time with her girlfriends, he brooded, obviously hurt by the rift and the glaring silence between them. Just by watching them throughout the evening, him waiting for her to look up and acknowledge him and her determination not to, their behaviour kept providing the lyrics until the song was written. Enjoyable evening; song done; time to go home. I never did hear if they overcame their issue. That song was *Silent Conversations*.

Silent Conversations

[Verse 1]
In a crowded room, yet I feel so alone,
Your eyes drift past me like a heart made of stone.
We sit on opposite sides of this empty space,
Words left unspoken, hidden from face.
I see the shadows of what we used to be,
But silence between us screams, can't you see?

[Chorus]
Oh, these silent conversations echo in the night,
Longing for your voice to set my heart alight.
Two souls in the dark can't find their way,
Through the whispers of love that we let slip away.

[Verse 2]
The clock ticks slowly, like a heartbeat on pause,
Memories of laughter now lost in the cause.
I reach out my hand but it's a fragile thread,
Hoping for magic, but it's all left unsaid.
You look right through me like I'm just a ghost,
In this haunted silence I miss you the most.

[Chorus]
Oh, these silent conversations echo in the night,
Longing for your voice to set my heart alight.
Two souls in the dark can't find their way,
Through the whispers of love that we let slip away.

[Bridge]
When did we stop sharing all our dreams?
Living in a world that's tearing at the seams.
Every glance feels heavy with what we won't say,
But I'm still here, love, hoping you'll find your way.

[Verse 3]
So turn to me now, let the silence break,
Let the walls crumble for our hearts' own sake.
I long for your laughter to fill up the room,
To chase away the shadows, to banish the gloom.

[Chorus]
Oh, these silent conversations echo in the night,
Longing for your voice to set my heart alight.
Two souls in the dark can't find their way,
Through the whispers of love that we let slip away.

[Outro]
So let's bridge this distance, let's find our way home,
In the language of love, we'll no longer roam.
For every silent moment, I'll fight to be free,
In these silent conversations, just you and me

***

And for a final consideration to spark your imagination, look at the heart-wrenching situations people find themselves in and how you can, maybe, draw attention to what some people have to cope with so there is a greater understanding of their plight.

Having watched friends and family go through the distressing ordeal of having a loved one suffer from Alzheimer's disease, and watching the movie *The Notebook*, and seeing the terrifying effects on the sufferer in the early stages when they become aware they are losing their memory, I really felt others should be aware of what it is like to go through that trauma. Hence my lyrics below, and how I try to capture the pain and distress of what it would be like to lose the threads of one's life until the whole image is gone from their mind.

Echoes of You

(Verse 1)
In the morning light, we rise anew,
Whispers of laughter in shades of blue.
Photographs scattered, a story untold,
Faded moments wrapped in gold.

(Chorus)
What is your name? I reach for the past,
A tapestry woven, but threads never last.
What is your name? I search in my mind,
As memories dance, leaving shadows behind.

(Verse 2)
Strolls down the lane, through seasons' embrace,
Echoes of joy, now a fleeting trace.
Hand in hand, we've weathered the years,
But the faces are blurring, lost in the tears.

(Chorus)
What is your name? I reach for the past,
A tapestry woven, but threads never last.
What is your name? I search in my mind,
As memories dance, leaving shadows behind.

(Bridge)
Through the silence, I'm calling for you,
In the twilight's embrace, our love feels so true.
But the whispers grow faint, the stories unwind,
As I hold onto you, while I'm losing my mind.

(Chorus)
What is your name? I reach for the past,
A tapestry woven, but threads never last.
What is your name? I search in my mind,
As memories dance, leaving shadows behind.

(Outro)
In the fading light, I'll hold you so dear,
With every last heartbeat, I'll keep you near.
Though the names may drift and the faces may fade,
In the heart of forever, our love won't be swayed.
What is your name? It echoes through time,
A melody sweet, though I'm losing my mind.

***

Finale

Hopefully, you have gained enough information from this brief guide on songwriting to get you started on your journey into the music industry. Take your time to perfect your lyrics, seek out like-minded creatives to share your creations with, and/or to collaborate with to put your lyrics to melodies and to share in the joy of success.

Keep a record of your lyrics/songs, the date they were written, and where you have distributed them, and keep a copy of the original drafts as evidence of your copyright to the material. Alternatively, post a copy of the handwritten lyrics and a USB drive of the recorded track or tracks to yourself via registered post, and file the envelope away without opening it.

Keep practising, keep collaborating and keep looking for that unique element in your music that will make you stand out.

And something to always keep in mind, which Jimmy Buffet expressed so succinctly:

Songwriters write songs,

but they really belong to the listener.

About the Author

Helen Iles is primarily a novelist, fiction story writer and poet. Turning her hand to writing song lyrics has opened new doors, including transforming children's stories into songs and then animated videos, further enhancing her skills. Always a lover of music, Helen focuses mainly on writing lyrics for Country music and Pop, and has released three albums in 2025 under her label *The Sound of Poetry*: *Lyrical Dream*, *These Country Boots*, and *The Gravity of Us*.

With many years of experience teaching creative writing, and with numerous books to her credit – including *Everything You Need to Know About … Writing Poetry – Simplified*, it was only a matter of time before *Everything You Need to Know About … Writing Songs – Simplified* followed in its wake.

www.ingramcontent.com/pod-product-compliance
Lightning Source LLC
Chambersburg PA
CBHW030331080526
44584CB00012B/818